Breath
The Invisible Power
behind
Health and Beauty

A Coaching Journey to Wholeness

Shant Joti J Maréchal

Copyright © 2015 Shant Joti J Maréchal
All rights reserved.

ISBN: 0993976905
ISBN 13: 9780993976902

the leaves are perfectly placed for a gentle climb
—

COVER ILLUSTRATION BY **OSHRI HAKAK,** www.LivingInkFlow.com

"As you breathe in, cherish yourself.
As you breathe out, cherish all Beings."
—Dalai Lama XIV

Thanks to my daughter, Jamie, for her teachings ever since her first day on earth.
Thank you to Guru Singh, Mikhail, Jim, Oshri, Jean-Yves, and my friend and editor, Nina Mongendre.

Table of Contents

To the Readers. xi

Introduction. xv

Part 1: The Coaching: How to Use This Book . . 1

Part 2: Forty-Day Coaching. 9

Part 3: Night Coaching 55

Part 4: Power of the Observer. 75

Part 5: The Powers behind Breath. 79

Part 6: My Experience with Breath 93

Part 7: Short Meditations to Reflect Upon. . . . 99

Part 8: Value of Health and Beauty,
For Centering Thoughts 107

Part 9: In Conclusion 117

Part 10: Journaling,
a writing journey to wholeness 119

To the Readers

The first step to any change is taken on the very day we start believing that our highest potential is within our reach.

This book is your coach. Open up to it; call on it. Question it; be honest and true. Carry it with you; write in it. Pick a page; and read a passage when you need to center yourself.

A good coach does not give you the answers but will help you find them.

These daily texts do not require the participation of the intellect; they speak to the heart. There is nothing to analyze. When the heart opens, we understand through love.

The coaching may seem repetitive; it is designed to be that way. Changing a thought pattern that prevents your vision from expanding so you can see the potential for a bigger life is changing a way to think that has become a habit. A habit cannot be eliminated in one day. It is a process;

let yourself move with elegance through this transformation.

This practice breaks down the blocks that interfere with reinventing yourself. You are not updating anything. You are not picking up pieces; you are starting anew. Let go. The heart likes playful and light communication. Smile, and lighten up. You are building a new life, with your eyes opening up to new horizons.

To support this process, I am including some texts that are designed to help you modify the way you look at food, because everything is food. We feed each other with words and with the expressions on our faces. We feed our hearts and minds with what we see, hear, and touch; with what we say and do; and with the choices we make. What we feed our body is in direct relation to what we feed our mind.

Do this test. For forty days, do not watch the news. Do not watch anything that weighs you down. Choose to watch some documentaries on nature, on the beauty of life! Watch videos of teachers who are working on unity, solutions, and healing. Turn all your free time into food for thought and for the heart. Stay away from everything that weighs the heart down. You will soon notice that your sleeping habits are changing and that your dreams will generate energy and life. Forty days is a blink of an eye in your lifetime. Live this experience fully to the end!

Choosing to do this training is not a challenge, and it is not a job for the intellect. It is an act of the *heart*. It is an act of love.

Introduction

It is an art to master breath. It is an art to master our thoughts. It is extremely important to build a relationship between breath and thoughts so that we can safely maintain our physical, mental, and spiritual capacities.

Thoughts have a direct impact on every facet of our lives. The collective thought currents permeate our minds easily unless we pay attention and maintain awareness of how we process our own thoughts. The outer currents are going very fast, and our social and working lives are based on the values that accompany the rhythms of those currents.

A tight relationship with our thoughts is one way to keep sight of our personal values, which become endangered if the values outside of ourselves become more important. When that happens, we drift along with the mental fuel coming from outside; we become unaware that our own values might not agree with our actions. We give up on our self-authority, our freedom of choice, to blindly follow the beat of the loudest drum.

Our relationship with our thoughts needs an anchor powerful enough to remind us of our inner world and all the powers that were invested in us. We need to keep healthy, creative, and loving thoughts alive.

Voluntary breathing is the perfect companion for thoughts. We can learn to relate to our thoughts and clean up the thought patterns that allow us to live only a small version of ourselves. We are missing something; we are missing this higher version of who we are.

Many try meditation and get discouraged or think that it is not for them. We are advised to let our thoughts drift, to watch them pass, and learn not to react to them. There are steps that we can take to get to the very blissful state of no thoughts. When our dark or negative thoughts are replaced by positive, creative ones, the dark thoughts do not haunt the mind anymore. This coaching is one way to work on that particular step. We replace the thought habit with a creative way of using our thoughts to support our choice to work on certain facets of ourselves. When haunting thoughts come back, we are then well equipped to deal creatively with them and not be disturbed by them. Meditation then becomes an exercise of the heart and not only of the mind. The heart is where all changes begin and grow.

Through voluntary, creative breathing, thought patterns become favorable. You have access to a positive and clear vision of all the choices that are available to you. You can claim your self-authority and use freedom of choice. This changes everything about the way you experience life.

Voluntary breathing is a practice that allows you to become conscious of your thought forms. Thought forms are the shape your thoughts take depending on your emotions or on your intention. What is your intention? Are you present in this moment or attached to an old emotion and letting your thoughts run wild in past events? Where are you going with your train of thoughts? Is it where you want to go…where you want to take others? Is it nice there? Is it a place where your own personal values are honored?

We have been told to measure our success and accomplishments according to a social or professional dream. Everything we do is about keeping up with the rules of that dream. We also have personal dreams. These are the dreams that we put to sleep, because our personal values often collide with those of the social or professional dream we chase every day, and this has become more important than our personal dream, hence more important than our own personal values. When we take some time out and center ourselves within our purpose, within our heart's calling, we can change the intention and create thought forms that fit our personal dream. Experiencing true joy in life depends on this coherence.

Conscious breathing takes us into this beautiful inner world where we can reclaim our own self-authority. We can create positive thought forms that change our perception of ourselves and the reality of the moment. As we practice using new, lighter, and more positive ways of thinking, our hearts set the beat for a new thought-processing habit.

What many are feeling—this desire to wake up—is the rising need for our personal dream to come alive, for our values to be heard. While breathing mindfully, we can listen to what these values have to say. A deep, voluntary inhale will give you the courage to respond so that they are heard by you first! Your response is what will change your relationship, with yourself first and then with all life.

When we stop denying our personal values, we start to experience a sense of freedom that is very healing physically, mentally, and spiritually. It is the awakening of the personal dream and the rising of the inner values that we have longed for. We find a sense of belonging.

This coaching awakens you to the depths of your values and to the roots that make you who you are. This is where you reach out to your personal dream, awaken it, and bring it to this side of life so you can empower it and manifest it.

When you get face-to-face with your life, there is a longing for something more, something meaningful that you will feel deeply in your heart. When breathing mindfully, you consciously connect to the soul that permeates everything. You transcend that longing into belonging, experiencing the plenitude that echoes your heart's calling.

As you breathe in with the intention to connect and exhale with the sound "om"—the closest sound that represents the infinite cosmic consciousness, God, Allah, Christ, Buddha, and Krishna—the vibration that this sounds creates echoes the eternal sound of the universe inside of you. You belong.

This coaching is about being awake and aware of this connection so you feel whole. Abundance dwells in wholeness, where we are never alone and where we are free.

As moments follow one another to create time, thoughts follow one another to create a constant inner dialogue that should support your dream.

Meditation is a state of no thoughts. In order to get there, we need to examine our way of processing thoughts. It is a habit of the mind; one thought leads to another and another, usually riding on some past-due emotion that takes over and governs a moment, a few hours, your day, or your life! Some of these emotions are stuck to you like glue but are really way overdue and should get on their merry way. Voluntary breathing is very powerful in helping you claim your time and your space into quiet stillness. There an overdue emotion will not find comfort in provoking a reaction, and it will disappear.

There is no need to fight your old habits and thought-processing ways, because any energy you invest in it only empowers it. Instead you will create a new habit, one that your old self-proclaimed "king and queen" emotions do not know!

Voluntary breathing allows presence. Outside events and opportunities will not go unnoticed or ignored in your life...opportunities you have passed by too often to reach success, to meet the right person, to do good deeds, or to help someone. So many times we are almost there, almost doing it. We dreamed of it; we wished for this. We ordered it, and when it comes, we miss the delivery by not being present and aware when it shows up.

This book will help you make it a habit to be present so you can greet the life-force that will lead you to a new relationship with yourself and with all life.

The first step is lifting your foot up to start the climb that will elevate you and give you a better perspective and a clearer vision of who you are and where you belong.

Take a deep breath!

Part 1
The Coaching: How to Use This Book

For a truly lasting change, one step at a time is the only way to get steady enough to pick up speed and maintain the course. Do it without thinking about it! Let your brain sleep, and wake up your heart! Keep it simple, and do it with joy.

1

> Wake up. Do not move very much, and pick up this book. Read it, starting with day one, put it down, and pretend you just woke up again, and focus mainly on your breath. Let the words you read descend into your heart, and create a picture in your mind; then apply the message you got from it. Let your imagination run free. Always end by connecting. Make this your first phone call of the day: *OM*.

2

Take a breather; take four. Set up four meetings a day (three minutes each) with voluntary, mindful breathing—one before each meal and one before sleep. These are three-minute beauty treatments for a healthy mind and a vibrant, beautiful, and powerful presence. Make these meetings a priority for forty days.

3

We remember 10 percent of what we read; 30 percent of what we see; 50 percent of what we see, hear, and write; 70 percent of what we discuss with others; and 80 percent of what we personally experience. Write a note at the end of this book right after you are done. It can be only a word that lit up a spark in your heart. Keep it light, and keep your eyes and ears open; you might just run across it during the day. Write only positive thoughts or feelings. Use another notebook if you need to write old-habit, negative thoughts; they need an outlet, but be brief. Do not give them energy, and do not dwell in the dark. Writing is very important in this process.

4

When you go to sleep, breathe very deeply and very slowly, and surf the waves of your breath. Go to part 3 of this book, pick a night whisper, or read a few, and meditate on it.

5

Any engagement in personal growth is a very intimate process, and, just as in alchemy, it needs to be contained like the lead in the crucible, so it turns into gold. Be intimate with your training and your progress; do your best, and enjoy the privacy of your own universe!

6

The only thing in this book that has a beginning and an end is the coaching. Browse freely through it.

7

Read about the powers often, and get familiar with the observer.

Voluntary breathing

There are very good books on the technical aspect of breath. Our goal for now is to develop a relationship with our breath.

For this first step, we want to keep it simple because voluntary, mindful breathing is a way to simplify our lives. There is no need to fill this book with biological matters that need to be studied or other techniques that need practice. This is important knowledge to acquire, but not all at once.

It has become difficult for many to believe in simple things. Simple things are somehow not associated with big results, and of course we need big results—and as fast as possible.

Well, one breath results in "life—now." You will not find bigger or faster results than that!

People are often very happy to get up and get on a fast train with the destination of "the end of the day." We have fashionable and cool ways to be the fastest on board; we can excel at multitasking, for example. People really believe that their attention is equally divided among all these things they do at once…and that they are so bright that they are functioning full tilt on gray matter. But gray is not a very bright color! That is not where life or happiness dwells. The heart has no space in that kind of mental activity because there is no time!

The awareness that you invest in the direction of your thoughts guides your presence. Voluntary breathing requires *presence,* and presence is a power that is under the law of universal connections.

When you get in the habit of voluntary, mindful breathing, you are going for the true sound of life, and you sing your own song. Managing your thoughts through voluntary breathing will change your attitude.

All this world needs is more love. Make sure that this is what you offer every day to your dear ones, to everyone you know and don't know.

So simple…such big results…so fast. Love always awakens a superior version of yourself.

Put your superior *self* and the quality of your life experience first on your priority list of values, and *breath* will become your most important asset.

Om

In my own practice, I explore the wild and untamed fields of my imagination. I journey into the unused potential human beings can access only by recognizing their infinite potential.

OM is a tool that acts as a key to open a door where human laws are overruled by universal and cosmic laws. It is the safest place to be, the place we long for. It is a place that we can feel for a brief moment but that is not in this world. We often look for this feeling of safety in our relationships or in a home and in material objects, but those things only provide a temporary relief from our yearning for our true home.

OM is the first vibration that we felt. It is the sound that we hear when we put the palms of our hands on our ears. It sounds about the same as when we are underwater. We hear the sound of our inner world. It is the sound we heard in the womb. The sound of a mother breathing is the source of life.

When we vibrate the sound OM, we go back to pure consciousness. We can heal our wounds and feed our heart from the cosmic soul current, where the laws are of divine order. We can be home.

Meditation:

We are made of stardust, we must assume our stardom.

OM TO WHOLENESS

If you do this meditation in the morning, sit up straight and elongate the spine. If you do it in the evening or before bed, lay down on your back on the floor.

Breathe deeply for a few minutes then cover your ears with the palm of your hands. Very gently, slightly press on the ears. Listen to the sound of your inner world. After a few minutes, focus your attention on the sound of your own breath. Inhale through your nose all the way down into your belly then exhale. Listen. The foetus you used to be depended on another's breath to feel secure. See the life force coming in through your own breath reaching down and filling every atom of your body with health. Feel that fresh air lighten up your heart and empowering the awareness of your infinite consciousness. Feel the communication between your inner universe and the cosmic universe.

Bring your hands to your knees and let them rest, palms down, if you are sitting up. Let your arms rest on either side of your body, palms down, if you are laying down.

Inhale deeply through the nose and exhale with the sound of OM. As you inhale, know that you are existing in the outer word, the same as any other cosmic body that is made of stardust. As you exhale assume your stardom. You are here to shine. OM is the union of all that you are: an infinite consciousness travelling through life.

Part 2
Forty-Day Coaching

A mindful breath and an inspired thought are the only tools you need to become an alchemist.

Day 1

Breathe in deeply…Just breathe, and feel yourself coming to life from deep inside. Exhale slowly. Stretch out, breathe in, and lift your arms straight up by your ears above your head, and stretch from fingers to toes. Stretch…stretch…exhale, and express your feeling…aaah…Breathe in deeply, and stretch out your whole body; hold the breath, stretch, stretch…Exhale gently, and repeat a few times.

Accept yourself. Be fine with where you are in your life. This is exactly where you have to start from. Voluntary breathing creates a direct link to a space inside that you must tend to, and you are the only one qualified for this job. Breathe…stay still. Feel and fill the moment with gratitude for the new life experience of this day.

Put on the half smile of the Buddha; it will keep your face muscles relaxed and your words kind…Stretch your body again…Smile.

Sit up straight, and connect: *Om*…as long as you want.

Reminder: Prioritize your meetings. Do not miss one of them. Breathe, smile, and take your time. If your half smile is gone, put it back on.

Day 2

Breathe in, and follow the air through your throat, through your diaphragm, and all the way down into your belly; hold the breath a few seconds, and exhale softly, emptying your belly, then your diaphragm, and out gently. Smile. Repeat. Inhale and stretch out, way out…Fill your belly, hold the position, and hold the breath for as long as you can while stretching even more. Gently let go, and always exhale slowly…aah, nice! Express yourself! Words are powerful.

The more you do it, the more you feel the emerging consciousness through your body. Come to the fetal position, and then stretch out and let out a big *aah*. Come to life. Feel your *self* rising up. Celebrate your heartbeat, and wake up to all that you are.

Let the universe hear you…*om*.

Day 3

Breathe in deeply, counting up to six or eight, whatever is comfortable for you, and exhale to the same count. Breathe through your nose. Repeat a few times. Then stretch and take a deep breath, and exhale with an *mmmm* sound. Tell your body, mind, and spirit: *mmmm…Om…*it is great to be *me*! *Om…*it is great to be *you*. *Om…*it is great to be *one*! *Om…*

Raise your values and expectations, and enjoy this day's new horizon. Visualize. Stretch into it. Take the time to appreciate all that you are. Express your love tenderly to your life, to your heart, to your *self…*

Stand up and breathe in as you stretch up! Up! Up! Feel the beauty and kindness of your heart. Make sure you share that today.

Your commitment to mindful breathing and the depth of your practice to improve health and beauty are equal to your interest in making the best out of this life. Breathe…Smile…Keep your eyes and your mind open to see more and more beauty. *Om…*

What message do you get out of these few moments? Sign in at the end of the book; write anything, or just draw a heart! Your response is imperative to the maintenance of your practice.

Day 4

Breathe through the nose. Do not move; just take in the air that is offered to you, and receive it with gratitude. Breathe deeply, slowly. Exhale gently to offer your own beauty as a gift to the universe.

Stretch, stretch…wake up gently; love who you are. Let your imagination take over. Create your own entrance into this day. Inhale, expand, receive, exhale, give…extend your life into all life.

Everything is allowed; you are completely free to be a bird flying in the blue sky or a wild horse running through a field of brightly colored flowers toward the sunrise. Breathe how it feels to be at the heart of your creation, and live it up all through the day. Create beauty in your environment; smile! Inhale and stretch into it; hold the position…Stretch out a little more…and exhale gently.

You have the power to feel all life, to be all life. Use your freedom to expand and include all life as yours; be *one* with all. Do not fear that much love…It is only a glimpse of what you are capable of! *Om…*

Day 5

Breathe deeply and softly through the nose. Visualize the sun rising. In order for you to really appreciate the sunrise, the fire inside you must also rise up from your heart. This warmth, this light, must consciously be invited to rise and awaken life in its purest form in every part of your body, mind, and spirit…as the sun does outside, for every living thing. Stretch out.

Breathe in the bright, warm sunlight, deep down into your belly. Exhale softly, and send healing and love to your entire day and to all beings that will be part of it.

This light inside keeps you warmhearted; it lets love, compassion, and healing flow and grow.

Stretch out while filling your body and heart with love for peace and harmony, and exhale softly. *Om*…

Breathe all this life in freely and gratefully. Lift someone today.

PS: Television and news—whether on TV, radio, the web, or in newspapers—are the main source of support for your old habit. How are you occupying your time without it? Note the documentaries you want to see, the research you want to do, the subjects you wish to explore…

Show up at your meetings. Keep up! See beauty in everyone and everything. It is all a reflection of you!

Day 6

Breathe deeply through the nose…All that matters right now is breath. This time is yours to salute and honor your life! Breathe…This is your highest priority. Breath is presence; presence contains the power to make this day a beautiful and bountiful one. Stretch out. Breathe; come into this moment and hold and cherish it. There is nothing but love right now. Stretch into that knowledge; imprint this message on every cell of your body.

Become present and aware of who you are. Your body is the highest-quality technology one could ever imagine! You are using a highly complex tool to experience this life. Your organic intelligence is pure perfection. Your respiratory system works with the circulatory system, which works with your cardiac, nervous, digestive systems…and on…and on. Trust that it knows better than you, and let it do its job. Give it a break from what it is you do to control or disturb its perfect ways, and only support it.

Breathe in how you see yourself at your best—physically, mentally, and spiritually. Stay hungry for health and beauty, and make one more step toward them! Stretch…again…Sit up…*Om*…

PS: Get familiar with "The Empowering Observer," part 4. Time to spice up this training. Keep up!

Day 7

Breathe…with joy, and smile. Go inside, inhale, and greet the creator of the coming day. It is *you*. You are the king or queen, sitting on the throne in the castle of your mind. Breathe powerfully in through the nose, and stretch as if you were to embrace the whole world and everyone you know, whether you like each person or not. Breathe deeply and accept it all as it is.

Stretch out into the realms of your powers. You rule over every word you say; be gentle in your own dialogue with your heart. Speak softly, speak consciously, and be kind to all you meet. Breathe…Stretch and reach out to your power of presence; own it with elegance and grace.

Breathe softly…Your thoughts, your actions, your words, and all of your being are meant to create beauty and health…It is all food! *Om*…all the way down to your heart…*om*…feel the joy…

Keep in the *light*! Keep a *light* heart! Eat *light*! And give *light*!

Day 8

Breathe…Feel the earth supporting you; feel the gravity anchoring you. Visualize the pressure, the friction, the stress, and the tensions that are at work inside of you, creating—with love—new cells…new thoughts…new life! The whole universe renews itself that way!

Stretch into this life activity. Everything has its place. Stress, pressure, tension, and friction are creative forces…You are a full-blown, beautiful universe with your own tools for creation.

Breathe all this in, and stretch out. Visualize the vibrating light pouring out of you…*Om*…

Today, be a healer. Speak words that bring light to others, and look only for beauty and kindness, and you will find only that. This is what love is all about; it is why it feels so good to be in love with life!

PS: How are your meetings going along? Maybe you could meet before meals…Make it easy on yourself to enjoy those moments. Say grace. Smile

Day 9

Breathe in deeply, and hold your breath. Enlarge your nostrils, and exhale, long and slow, through your nose. Continue...

Stretch out. Open your heart, and listen as it tells you how grateful it is for your support. Stay connected. Your heart is alive and playing its drum for you. Dance through your life experience today; let your heart sing.

Have you met with ambivalence yet? It speaks to you as an old friend would. Its favorite words are: I'm not sure...just today...not today, maybe tomorrow...This won't work...When you clean house some of the old emotions and painful memories that you have been dragging along want to remain in your life. This causes ambivalence.

Be present. If ambivalence wants to play, then play, but make sure you make the rules! It comes for a good reason...Find your power of self-authority and be fully in charge. Be a good host, but do not keep this guest too long. *Om*...

Now stretch more than you ever have. You just made a friend of what would once have knocked you over! Celebrate! Keep up! Smile.

PS: Have you browsed through this book yet? Read about the observer, part 4. How is your relationship with your observer? For the next few days, be particularly aware of this. What makes you want to react? Have you noticed anything about your attitude? Have you tried breathing… and staying still instead of reacting?

Write about it.

Day 10

Wake up. Put your smile on right away. Breathe in down to your belly; fill it up, and let thoughts of an emerald-green waterfall flow through your very strong and powerful heart. Exhale; let the air out. Join hands, and rub them together until warm. Get the blood flowing. Rub your face, and breathe in very deeply through the nose. Stretch out...

You know where you are heading. You have the power to get there smiling. This will make the difference whether you enjoy the ride or not. Breathe in deeply your strength of character, and hold the breath as the air fills up each and every blood cell with power and love. Feel it circulate in your veins! This is the river of your life! Every river heads for the ocean. Row your way with meaningful breaths toward your goal.

This is an intimate exploration of your inner strength and beauty, of your precious gifts. *Om*...

PS: Show up at your meetings. Bring back this feeling, and let your heart be free to embrace life.

Day 11

Take your first voluntary breath of the day. Salute, and welcome your loving *self*…your angel…God…*Om*…

Stretch out every muscle inside your skin. Enjoy deeply this stretch-out routine! Stand up, and reach up to the sky with your fingers…up, up, up! Breathe…Smile…Reach down to the ground, make a reverence, and honor your life. Breathe… Think "life is good"…Say it out loud!

Reach to the east with both arms, and dive into the life-force of the sunrise. Reach to the west, and feel the peaceful essence of a sunset settle your mind on a bright-orange horizon. Become aware of your beauty. Stay present to it. Be sure of it. Hold the thought throughout the day. Lift yourself up; *you are beautiful*! Lift others! *Om*…

PS: Make a mental picture from this text, and bring it to mind when you take your first voluntary breaths during your meetings today. Repeat, "I am beautiful" as you see your soul in the sunset.

Day 12

Breathe…This journey is working out. You now have a quest. You are not just going forward, you are heading in your own direction.

Stretch, and appreciate the changes that are happening now, in the first moments of your day. Breathe out and enjoy your adventure. Smile, and express your joy. Stretch out. Involve your loved ones; visualize their faces with a great smile and their hearts filled with joy, and stretch…Breathe in deeply with the firm belief that all is well; all is in order.

Deep, deep breathing…let the soul of all life fill your heart with love. The picture is changing; new colors are appearing in your life, brighter and softer. Remember, you are the artist, and your life is a canvas. Go slowly, reflect, and let yourself be inspired. Look deeply in search of beauty—the deeper the more stunning! Be what you want to see. *Om*…

PS: Did you read about the powers available to you through voluntary breathing? Practice the power of flexibility. Drink water and reflect on the life that enters your body as you swallow. Flexibility allows grace in the movements of the body and movements of the mind. Bring a fluid approach to your words and gestures. Be flexible to, but firmly stand your ground. Wear your half smile humbly, and practice flexibility.

Day 13

Hey *you*! Good morning! Breathe…Smile…Stretch out! Breathe in through your nose, taking in the air for two seconds. Fill your belly, hold two seconds, and breathe out two seconds. Do this a few times, and listen to your breath; this is the train of your life passing. Rise up and catch it!

Now go to the mirror, smile, and very, very softly say, "Hey *you*!" Welcome your *self*. Be aware of the goodness of your heart, and be grateful. Welcome this day. Feel the whole world opening for you. When you greet your *self* you greet your angel. You invite the divine part of yourself to be part of your day.

Today is all about the beauty and ethics of living a great life. Breathe.

If your goal is to lose weight, take the weight off your heart. It will change the size of your love, and that will change the size of your clothes. This is what authenticity is all about. You can love everything about yourself. Your heart does! *Om*…

PS: Become aware of your relationship with yourself. Be kind to your heart, but work hard on yourself. Smile compassionately. Breathe…Hold your angel's hand.

Day 14

Breathe; make your own breathe-and-stretch creation this morning. Be constant with breath. Let yourself go into the place of your dream. If you don't know your dream, dream one up!

Your *self* knows what you are capable of, so raise your expectations. Expect the best! Do not stop at failures…You are missing the main part of your learning experience. Do not go back and start from the beginning; pick yourself up, and rise up to meet these expectations!

Breathe…Your relationship with yourself is becoming richer as your knowledge of who you really are grows.

Make it easy on yourself. Apply what you know, but keep learning. Be grateful…Be graceful…Be beautiful! Breathe…Smile. *Om*…

PS: How are your meetings? Take a moment right in the midst of a conversation to bring your awareness to your breath. Look at the person who is in front of you breathe. Become more present to breath as life.

Day 15

Breathe normally; do not move. Just feel the air as you breathe in, and let it out. Be very conscious of your participation in the creation of your life today, in the way this day will unfold. Breathe, and purposely direct the air to your chi, the center of vitality, for a great, radiant, and beautiful energy you can share all day.

Observe the changes in your relationships to people, to nature, and to food. Wear the half smile of the Buddha; it is food for your heart and for your mind, as well as for everyone in your life.

You are more and more present to all that lifts, and more and more detached from all that weighs.

Breathe, hold the breath, and stretch…

Breathe deeply…Think of beauty. Think of nature. Think of gardens and flowers. Think of animals, wild and free and domestic ones, roaming in the fields. Think of spring and all the babies feeding from their mothers' milk and lying close for an afternoon siesta. Breathe with them!

Today, start supporting your perfectly designed human body. Eat fresh, beautiful, live food.

The body hears what we pretend not to know about the food we take in. This voluntary ignorance creates an inner incoherence that is more harmful than a simple and honest agreement with your truly honest opinion, whatever it is. But make sure you are well informed. Food illiteracy is not an option in your quest for authenticity.

You are going through a process that will demand truly responsible choices. Beauty lives in the truth. Ignorance does not mean that you don't know, it means to know and pretend that you do not. Happiness does not pretend.

Courageously get informed, and make your own inventory of pros and cons of the way you support your physical, mental, and emotional body. Food deals with all of these facets of our being. Get informed, and check out whether you support nature or not and life. You know the truth. Breathe; act upon what you know and what you believe in. Stand tall and true. *Om*...

Day 16

Breathe and stretch out. Keep your eyes closed, and repeat—stretch, stretch...Let go slowly. You are a garden of fragile flowers with powerful perfumes. Respect both powers!

Breathe powerfully. Stretch out. Stand up. Lift your arms as you inhale life, and let them down gently as you exhale. Visualize that with any problems, you can fly through them! Take a deep breath, and raise your spirit as if it has wings. Raise your arms. Enter that one moment that will change your day. Take a deep breath. *Om*...Stand up and continue this exercise. Breathe in as you lift the arms up, and exhale as you bring them down. Be elegant...Be at peace...Be the dove.

While you are taking time off from television and news, allow space for new knowledge about the good things that will enhance your life, and perfume your days with good news, music, dance and joy.

Watch documentaries on foods of the world... on great achievers, masters. See their absolute faith in what they believe in. Explore God's pharmacy, herbs and spices, and make sure to learn something every day. Breathe...Smile...Take a conscious breath between each bite...Take notes.

You are what you eat! Be beautiful!

Day 17

Breathe in the morning energy that awakens all life. Feel the river of your life, the river of your days, the river of your thoughts, the river of your love. Stretch out into it. Water is flexible. All rivers go to the ocean. They always find their way. Keep your dream flowing. Breathe in with faith, and stretch into the land of your highest potential. Let your breath out as gently as you would kiss a child. Breath is your embrace to all life.

From now on, double up the amount of water you drink. Buy yourself a water bottle. Add some orange flower water or rose water, just a few drops. Try some cucumber or ginger slices in it. Drink up, and visualize your river…Let it flow through your heart, all through the day. Water the seed of love that was planted in your heart; love your life! *Om…*

PS: In your meetings, feel the river of your life run down the mountain of your mental and emotional stability where your values are anchored. Feel the powerful flow of life empower these values, and be grateful. Breathe.

Day 18

Stay still, and breathe normally. Move your toes and your hands, stretch your neck, and take a long deep breath in as you press the back of your neck on your pillow. Hold it, and stretch your whole body. Elongate your spine, and stretch. Exhale slowly, and relax for a few moments. Repeat, and feel your heart open like a beautiful blue morning glory.

These flowers are such an inspiration. They grow all rolled up, and one morning they twist themselves open, for one day only.

Open your mind very wide, and breathe a pure, fresh, new day. A deep transformation has begun. Keep up! Do everything responsibly. Eat healthy, and speak healthy words in your dialogue with yourself and with others. Today accept everything as it is—no judgment, no critique, with peace and freedom all around.

Let nature inspire you. Be a morning glory; untwist yourself wide open, and show your inner beauty as if you only had this one day. Breathe dearly. *Om…*

PS: Use time during your meetings with breath to communicate with your observer. You want to be active, not reactive. Listen; the observer echoes your heart's values so that you can belong.

Day 19

Inhale with joy! Is this working? Are you smiling this morning? Be grateful for the opportunity to create a great day for yourself. A great day is a day in which you discover more and more beauty and potential in yourself and see the potential in others and all the world around.

Stretch into that potential, and reach out! Keep your eyes open to see the opportunities that show up. Say yes when they do, and zoom in on that potential.

Breathe…Use humor…Don't be a grouch… Grouches do not learn; they whine. Enjoy who you are fully, and go for it.

Be playful with your practice, and watch other people breathe and use breath to unite, breathe along. *Om*…

PS: Create an opportunity to give to someone, however big or small, giving is receiving.

Day 20

Breathe deeply. Life-force is moving in. Be a perfect host; welcome this powerful gentleness. Express your wish to support and maintain the perfect balance it is offering you. Breathe… Stretch…Smile…Sing!

Breathe deeply all the way down to your chi, and with your eyes closed, set your vision in the middle of your eyebrows. Set your mind on your highest values, and set your heart on love.

Breathe in. Receive the air, and forcefully breathe out. Repeat for a few minutes.

Feel the weight lifting off your heart as you exhale…You are as stable as a mountain, no need for any extra weight. Keep a light heart. Love is weightless; it lifts you up. There are great treasures in the breezy flow of mindful breathing. *Om…*

Day 21

Breathe slowly, deeply. Get up, inhale, and stretch up, up, up. Move slowly with your breath… Breathe. Invite your angel or your divine energy to be part of your life today.

Breathe with the life-force guiding your moves. Put your foot on the floor gently, and slowly—from heel to toe—feel the ground. Feel the support from the earth, and feel your weight resting on this one foot as you go on to the next step. Walk and breathe this way for a few minutes; then come to a stop. Inhale, suspend the breath, and stretch out. Exhale—feet together, hold your hands in front of you palms up—and receive the abundant flow of life.

On this day you are as stable as a mountain. Breathe…Smile…Any challenge is equal to your capacity, so be OK with it.

Just breathe, and breeze through it all. *Om…*

Day 22

Breathe…Inhale as if you were greeting a master teacher. Humbly exhale with respect. A great teacher can only help you open your eyes and your mind wider, so you can find your own answer in the vast fields of wisdom inside of you. Expect the answer to come from there, from your teacher inside not from someone else. Another's answer fits another's plans. Breathe, and open your heart, your mind, and your eyes to the infinite possibilities of life. Be present to your humble teacher's guidance. He speaks softly; stay still.

You may ask a thousand people the true meaning of humility, but few people know. The only way to know humility is to be OK with not knowing and just keep your quest alive. Do not take another's knowledge for your own.

Breathe the winds of higher knowledge that are welcoming you to a life where everything is possible. Breathe the freedom of exploring your world without any frontiers. Stretch out…Let go gently. The answer always comes. *Om*…

PS: Get more and more familiar with the powers. Practice the one that is most demanding, and see which one is most helpful. Take notes.

Day 23

Breathe and stretch...Let out the air, and whisper, "Thank you." Do it again. Awaken your heart to the poetry of life and the harmony of all living things. Stretch out, and exhale with ease and gratitude.

Stand up, stretch up, and take a few steps. Reach way high. As you progress with this training, let the *self* make the corrections when need be. Keep up! Breathe cool air!

Being conscious, fully conscious, does not mean that we always act according to our highest values; it means that we can see and know where we could do better. We kindly accept our deficiencies and apply what we learned next time.

Notice the joy and the strong presence of the child who just learned something. Look at that smile! That is the smile to wear today! Inhale this state of innocence. You are here to learn about life! Respect all forms of life. *Om*...

Bless your life! Breathe...

Day 24

Breathe…Stretch…Come to consciousness with a beautiful inner dialogue:

"I feed my creative thoughts. I invest all my love in going forward, and I expect the best to come toward me. I rise up to the more open fields where blessings come in many disguises, and I use my self-authority to declare anything that comes to me a blessing.

"I breathe in my experience of life as I sail through to wider horizons. Anything that happens today, I can deal with as it happens, when it happens.

"A nice, long, deep, voluntary breath will get me through anything and show me the way through any block. I can heal anything right then and there, the moment it happens."

Breathe in this confidence, and use it. *Om*…

PS: Don't forget your meetings.

Day 25

Breathe…Acknowledge that you are intentionally breathing. You are using your self-authority. You can inhale respect and joy; you can inhale courage and bravery. Acknowledge the full intention that flows through your breath. What you need… breathe it!

Rise and greet your *self* with wide-open arms. Open your heart to everything and everyone, knowing that you are the master of your life.

The changes taking place will let themselves be known to you by suggesting new ethics of conduct and new ways to speak, to see, to hear, and to feel life's currents.

Be present. Be flexible. Engage in the changes actively. Take a few good breaths and respond consciously. *Om…*

Work with your observer. When you do great, celebrate!

Day 26

Breathe…Believe in what you do. You are healthy. Your body is alert, and all the parts are functioning properly right now. Your mind is sound, and your spirit is in full flight to a healthier and more beautiful and powerful you!

A gentle soul heals emotional pain. Breathe… Emotions are part of this busy life…They show up all excited, disturbing whatever you are doing. Gently respect the message they bring, and set them free. Remember you are not alone. You are with the soul of life!

Train your emotional body as you train your breath…Keep doing what you are doing… Go with what matters and what supports you. Everything will find its way to what it was meant to be.

Breathe. Smile through it…Be a silent teacher, breathe deeply, and watch the world slow down. *Om…*

Day 27

Breathe deeply and quietly for a few minutes. Sit up. Breathe deeper.

Rub your hands together for at least one minute; start that spark inside, in your heart. Let the fire ignite every cell of your body. Feel the fiery light in your mind activating bright, warm, favorable thoughts.

Take a deep breath now. Breathe in, and stretch your arms up…way up there. Breathe out, and bring them slowly back down, reaching as far as you can with your fingers on each side as you paint a rainbow of warm love above you…Do this ever so slowly; reach out, stretch your arms, hands, and fingers up, palms up, and lift that love out to the infinite. Turn your palms down, and bring all that love down to your heart. Close your eyes, and share it with all the people who need it in this world.

Repeat for ten minutes as you breathe deeply, and let your fire brighten up this rainbow that is your light within, shining through space and time. Breathe and empower your energy field. Shine through the day! *Om*…breathe. Smile!

Day 28

Breathe…Rise and smile. Stretch up! You are a human being in full evolution. Stand up, and spread your feet apart shoulder width, feet are parallel, and knees are slightly bent. Powerfully anchor your feet to the ground; grow roots. Breathe deeply, and go deeper into the earth. Empower yourself; energize yourself. Breathe deeply, and smile.

Put your hands on your heart and then open your arms and your heart as you inhale. Stretch them out on either side. Greet your day with a warm welcome. Exhale and bring your hands back to your heart. Repeat a few times.

Honor your participation in your evolution; honor your efforts by blessing every grand or every humble step you take on your way. *Om*…

PS: During your meetings with breath, do this exercise, and also do it mentally a few times today. Breathe, and smile at yourself.

Day 29

Breathe…Smile…Stretch out. Breathe deeply, and come to this new day with radiance and joy.

The universe needs you to be clear because it answers to the energies that you put out. Take a deep breath, and go inside to tune in to your values. Refine yourself, and make a clear statement of what matters to you.

The body asks that you be very clear minded and conscious, present to the spirit that provides you with the elegance and grace of movement. The power of stability is your greatest asset in the midst of change. It is for you to develop that skill and to bring it on strong.

Yoga means union. Keeping a yoga position is a perfect exchange between body, mind, and spirit. Sit up, and put your arms up, palms facing each other. Breathe normally, and hold the position one to three minutes. When tired, stretch up a little more. Concentrate on breath if pain comes. Learn about tolerance and perseverance. Be fully aware of your self-authority. Use that power over yourself.

Slowly put your arms down without whining. Let your body hear you say *yes* as you gently exhale. Learn to see success in everything that you achieve.

PS: Have a mental meeting with breath a few more times a day. Set up a time or a simple reminder in your work place. Continue whatever you are doing, and intentionally breathe and center yourself. Go to what matters; look into your heart. Smile.

Day 30

Breathe. Congratulations…this has become a habit—better than the one before! You are waking up happier for no reason at all. Breathe your success; breathe victory!

When intention becomes natural, then ease sets in.

Breathe…Stay in stillness…Get familiar with being happy and being still…This is your sacred place. There is only breath, stillness, and happiness in your life right now. Breathe as if you are in the most wonderfully scented flower garden…Do not move; just delight yourself.

This is the artist's studio where you create your day. This is the source of the genius creator. This is where your colors are the brightest!

Breathe and bathe in this moment of creation. Paint your day, and leave space for any unexpected events on your daily canvas. All events will come to you so that you can master your art. Open your mind and your heart, and accept what comes your way. Be grateful! Breathe…Smile… *Om…*

Day 31

Rise up. Breathe nice, long, and deep breaths… Stand up with your back against a wall, and stretch up. Make yourself as tall as you can. Feel your spine straightening up. Push lightly against the wall with your lower back, and stay in this perfect position for a minute. Breathe deeply.

Starting today, as you continue your conscious breathing practice, be happy that you are elevating your commitment and engaging in this new life. The results will be equal to the efforts you put in! The benefits are equal to your investment. You are on your way to great spiritual health and beauty.

Feel the change already. Take time; take your time. Elongate your spine, and breathe yourself back to stillness…often. Smile. *Om*…

Take more notes from now on. Write how you feel. Write the goals that come to mind. Write about how you have used presence and other powers. How about detachment? Detach yourself from everything else, and write.

Day 32

Breathe, stretch, and smile, and then come down to the floor, and sit with your back very straight. Elongate the spine.

Close your eyes, and press your hands together in front of your heart. Inhale deeply...*Om*...Let the air out gently through the nose, and feel the vibration of your voice inside your heart. Put on your half smile. Take a very deep breath, exhale, and let this sound resonate inside you as long as you can. Be a cavern, and see your deepest treasures radiate light in all your cells; this is a healing exercise. Create a very peaceful place. Breathe deeply. Be aware of the sweet centering that is happening inside. This is the pure power of breath uniting heart, mind, and spirit. Three minutes.

Concentrate on breath. Lift your arms parallel to the floor, and hold the position. If it becomes too much, turn your palms face up for a few seconds, then inhale powerfully, and resume the position.

Loosen your shoulders, and rotate your head. Repeat the sound *om*, and this time feel your vibration tuning in to the universal sound. This is a prayer...an offering. No demand—you already have everything you need.

Day 33

Maintain the voluntary breathing and stretching routine. By now, you certainly have a favorite way to go about it. That is great! Excellent! Keep it up, and enhance it your own way, as long as breath is the center of your attention. Do not forget the half smile. It is the foundation of your attitude of gratitude.

Stand on your two feet, and fix your eyes on a point at the horizon. Lift your hands, palms facing down, and use them as weights to help keep your balance. Put your right foot on top of the left one, any way you feel comfortable. Stand on one leg for one minute, and then change feet. Stand one minute. Breathe normally through this exercise, and continue to fix a dot on the horizon or on a wall. This exercise will help you keep your mind stable and will bring grace to your body movements through the day. *Om*.

You can repeat this exercise during your meetings with breath.

Mindful breathing awakens consciousness of perception. Observe yourself today. Do you have a favorable perception of yourself…of others…of your work? Be a favorable spirit for everything and everyone…Smile…*Om*…

PS: How are you doing with food? It takes courage to investigate and recognize that humanitarian values are often distorted, and divine values are absent. Feed your mind with truth and honesty. Do some research on sustainable projects, on people working on powerful solutions. Participate by making adequate choices in your own lifestyle, for better health and beauty for all.

Day 34

Notice that you wake up now conscious of your breathing. Notice the celebration feeling as you welcome the day…Isn't this grand? This started with a choice you made: "I'm going to do this." And another one followed it: to persevere every morning to support your choice. Every morning, for the rest of your life, you will refine the part you play as cocreator of life, of joy, and peace. Join others who care, get involved, and make this world a better place for somebody, each day.

Notice how you are now entering with ease into the change that is happening. This is true transformation! It is accomplished with sweet maturity, grace, and excellence. Feel the bliss and rejoice.

Today, stay aware of all the small decisions you make, and check out what bigger intention they support. You might be surprised by the ease with which you are starting to eliminate some choices as new ones become possible!

Now sit on the ground, elongate your spine, and move your shoulders up and down for one minute. Rotate your head clockwise for one minute and counterclockwise another minute. Breathe deeply, and center yourself. Inhale…Exhale…*Om*…Feel the cavern-like echo inside your body. Feel your heart drum carrying out your sound, and tune in with all *life*!

Day 35

Breathe. Meet your life! Hear the whisper of your breath; this is spirit flowing through. Rise up, and keep with the melody of your own rhythm, with the waves of breath. Imagine that you are composing your own masterpiece, and you are creating it with the greatest music producer; your whole universe is playing.

Tune your body. Stretch up, and reach up the highest you can. See each vertebra as a keynote you are tuning on a beautiful piano! Bend down from the bottom of the spine, and feel each vertebra as you bring your hands to the floor. Feel your breath like you would a flute echoing through valleys and mountains.

All that you do, all that you speak, see, hear, and touch will be mixed and remixed to transform into your new *life*! *Om*…

Offer the world your masterpiece. Be glorious. Breathe; smile.

PS: Today, observe how you can maintain your song through any event. Pay attention to your posture and your speech. Stand up, and stand tall. Speak softly.

Day 36

Breathe gently, with respect to all life. Invite love in every breath, and share it. You can heal everything with love, and if it does not work, increase the dosage. Breathe, and bring your presence into the moment.

This is a breath and thought coaching. This will take you inside your mind, where beautiful thoughts are waiting for you to breathe them into your heart and into your whole body. Free these thoughts as they reveal your deepest intent. Breathe into this creation, and your intention will come to you freely—no restriction, no small or big emotion, no thought to hold on to. Let go, and breathe your beautiful heart out!

This determination is effortless. Step on that first step, and breathe every morning, every day. Always make contact with the breath first. This is life, health, and beauty taking you to second and third steps and on to your path as the day unfolds. But each day starts on the first step; breathe your first breath with gratitude.

Be aware that thoughts go straight to the heart and that what you think becomes real. It is guaranteed. So have favorable thoughts, for yourself and for others. *Om…*

Day 37

Breathe…Imagine an apple tree. See its beautiful, white flowers in the spring. See the green leaves fill up the branches and the apples start to grow in summer, and imagine you pick one, a ripe, red, juicy apple…Bite into it. Breathe every sensation this visualization contains.

Feel the life in it, eat it to the core, and take out a seed. In this seed is a new tree with flowers, leaves, and apples. The seed's intention is to be a tree. See the tree in the seed.

The intention for human beings is to mold their inner universe to the cosmic divine consciousness to let the spiritual being experience life in the material world. This means to love and care for all nature and each other, to learn from our children and become better teachers for them…to do our very best to make this world a better place.

See this intention in everyone. Keep your mind clean and clear, and your true beauty will emerge from a radiant glow of love.

Surrender to who you are…to your divine intention. Breathe…You are beautiful.

Rise, and create a personal stretching routine. Breathe; smile. *Om*…

Day 38

Wake up, and breathe consciously; life is starting around you and for you, at this very moment. Be aware that you inhale to live a great moment… the moment that is offered to you *now*. Be conscious of your relationship with the higher being inside, your loving self, your angel self. You are reaching a sixth sense. You see through things and people; you see the deeper sense of life. It is the most profound capacity of your mind's eye to see the source of all things.

Breathe, and make sure to pay attention to how you look at people; see beauty, bravery, and courage. See the longing for love, and give love so they belong. See love in their eyes. It is there if you give them love! Allow yourself to share your presence, and be fully aware of your breath in those moments. Enjoy the lightness and the transparency.

Breathe, and stretch out; elongate the spine. Rise up, and reach up to the sky with wide-open hands, and offer yourself; offer your day. Bring your arms down slowly. Stand firmly on both feet, and put your hands one over the other, palms up in front of your heart to receive the gift of today with gratitude. *Om*…

Day 39

Breathe…Rise up inhaling air that you transform as food for your blood, oxygenating every part of your body…Exhale with deep thanks for this experience. Inhale light, a full spectrum of the rainbow that already exists in your heart. Stand up, spread your feet apart shoulder width, and stretch your arms out on each side with palms facing up…Breathe, and balance these rays of light from one hand to the other. Visualize. Accept this treasure; it is yours to hold and to share. It is your job to see that it keeps shining.

This light comes directly from your innate radiance. The love in the center of your heart rises up to your perfectly clear mind to generate colorful thoughts that fill the empty spaces and enlighten the dark ones in the perception you have of your life.

Breathe light that awakens your faith in yourself and in others. Breathe beauty…Breathe friendship. The imagination is where all the scenarios of life are written. Visualize; go in this world of creation, and write a scenario that will become the life you want. *Om*…

The alchemy is happening. Breathe deeply…Be lighthearted…Keep up your meetings with *self*, and give yourself credit!

Day 40

Breathe; celebrate your life. Breathe, and let your mind go empty. Just breathe…now. Say yes to your creations. Say yes to your life as you see it and build it. Say yes to your talents. Say yes to your deficiencies, and delegate. Trust! Learn!

Acknowledge that your attitude toward the coming day, people, and life in general has taken a turn. This journey is not over; the changes are ongoing. It is now your responsibility to maintain and engage deeper toward a healthy body, healthy mind, and healthy beauty.

Get a book on the science of breath. Add another fulfilling ingredient to your daily life—yoga, martial arts, juggling, walking…whatever suits you. Join a class, and meet people who are headed in the same direction you are.

Breathe. Make notes every day in your agenda to remind you to start each chore with a few mindful breaths. Stay in touch with your *self*.

This first step, taken every day, supports the success of any other change you might want to make. Nutrition, weight loss, healing, relationships—they can all be worked out with breath.

Breathe, and always, always keep the half smile.

Bless your heart…Bless your loved ones…and let the beauty of your soul shine through.

Part 3
Night Coaching
Whispers of the Heart

During the day the mind is solicited from right and left. The brain registers messages without our consent, and all of a sudden, when we slow down, all this stuff shows up as thoughts, and we have no idea where they come from! They can invade our mind and affect the quality of sleep.

Going to sleep is a surrender. It is very important to clear out all pressure and tension from your mental activities and dive with complete trust and faith into a peaceful night.

The night whispers have been designed to send you off into a regenerative sleep where your intuitive capacities reach out to the realms of dreams that will guide and support your evolution.

You do not have to follow day to day. You can pick one randomly and let it sink in your mind.

You can read a few and let them paint a picture for you to drift into the night.

Are you inhaling air way down into your belly, then your diaphragm, then your upper chest? Are you exhaling by reversing the process? Sounds awkward? This is the way to breathe properly. Practice breathing lying down, and feel the wave. Breathe deeply, slowly. Let your angel take over...

1

Listen to your breath, and mindfully let the flow of life empower all that you have invested in your day. Trust in this time of sweet surrender. Breathe nice and slow…Keep your half smile on…

2

Close your eyes, and repeat: My awareness of breath is the source that feeds my heart and my thoughts.
Inhale love into your heart, and exhale softly as your whole being radiates the pure essence of your true self into the night…

3

Follow the waves of your breath landing on a white, sandy beach by the turquoise, crystal-clear water…Go to your dream, and prepare to bring it back on this side of life soon! Deep, deep breaths…

4

Breathe…Surrender…Feel the victory in your breath. Victory needs to be enjoyed and celebrated. Smile, and go to your inner self with the good news that you are giving it a place of choice in your life.

5

Inhale the perfect bliss of plenitude and simplicity. Breathe in as your eyes close on this perfect day, and exhale contentment and gratitude. Believe that, somehow, all is in order, and it is not for you to always understand life's ways. It might not seem in order, but it is…

6

Breathe…Feel the support of the earth. Feel the gravity that comes to help you relax every muscle, nerve, and organ of your body. Feel the stability in your biological systems. Enjoy a mental clarity and a quiet spirit. Breathe in this blessing…Breathe out your gratitude… Keep with your breath as you let go…

7

Breathe…Bring your mind down to one thought…Slow down…Go into stillness… Breathe, and listen to your deep inhaling as if you are on a beach and a beautiful, warm wave of turquoise water comes up to massage your whole body. As it rolls back to the ocean, you feel your body molding itself into the warm sand…into stillness. Breathe…Sleep.

8

Listen to your breath, and drift away with a nice, soft wind under your wings, heading toward a wide horizon where you will lay yourself down as an offering…

9

Close your eyes, and start deep breathing. Bring your awareness to your superior *self*, the one who loves you, knows you, and knows your destiny. Lay down your worries; trust that everything will be fine. Put on the half smile, and breathe gently…

10

Smile, and see from one step up all that passes through your mind. Let it go, leaving no trace. Inhale deep and long. What occupies your mind are miscellaneous thoughts in the bigger plan. Breathe in the divine intention that was set for you, and trust. You are fully protected; let go…

11

Breathe deeply; direct your thoughts toward health and beauty. Express gratitude to your vital life-force. Be grateful for who you are, for getting stronger and more beautiful as you discover your true self. Leave this day smiling. Breathe softly…

12

Breathe, and enjoy these moments of surrender…no plans…no expectations…nothing…just breathe…

13

Be proud to support the harmony between your needs and the food you choose to keep them satisfied! Breathe, and empower yourself…This can be done gently…very gently. Sleep is great food for body, mind, and spirit. Empower your quietude with a smile and breathe…

14

Breathe, and fill your whole body—every atom of every cell—with pure, fresh oxygen. Send love to every part of your body,

and pour gratitude over your beautiful
heart. Love this sleep time! Breathe…

15

Breathe…Walk into the night, and aim toward
a fully regenerative and rejuvenating experience that will prepare you for a wonderful
awakening! Breathe.…Walk on…Breathe…

16

Lying on your bed, straighten your spine, tuck
in your chin a little, and stretch the back of
your neck. Press down on your bed with the
back of your head as you exhale. (No pillow
is best.) Keep a regular rhythm, and continue
this for a minute or two. You might not move
at all for the whole night…Breathe deeply.

17

Lie on your back, and elongate your spine;
breathe deeply. Inhale…Exhale…Feel the air pass
through your nostrils. Feel it go down through
your throat, your diaphragm, and into your belly.
Let your belly rise. Exhale the same way…Let the
air out first through your nostrils, your throat, your
diaphragm, and empty your belly. This creates
a wave as if the air was water going inside your

belly, as if your chi was a beach…and coming back out into an ocean of air. Let the center of your energy, your chi, be completely relaxed. Breathe…

18

Breathe…nice and smooth. Just be comfortable, lie on your back, and be happy. Touch your thumbs and your index fingers together to form a heart, and rest your hands on your belly. Let the universe know that this life is loved and cared for…Smile…Breathe…Sleep…

19

Breathe, visualize, and create powerful thoughts of gratitude. Favorable thoughts are healing. Use your breath to keep generating them. Empower your self-authority. You are completely free to sleep now…

20

Chanting is a great way to train your breath to dance with your heart! *Om* yourself to sleep…

21

Your *self* is beautiful. It is your eternal consciousness, and it lives in your eternal reality. Put down all fences, and let yourself go… Breathe…Listen to your breath…Let go…

22

Breathe…Turn the present around moment by moment, breath by breath. Acknowledge how powerful this skill is becoming in your life. Feel the strong support it creates for each step you take on your way to a greater life. Feel the support of the earth…Feel how blessed you are…right now…Breathe…Smile…

23

Breathe…Each day is but a blink of an eye. Sleep so you can be awake and present when it happens. Breathe…

24

Breathe…The changes you want will present themselves to you when you live up to what you stand for. Go get your dream…Breathe deeply… Create…What is the color of your dream?

Visualize, reach out, and create in the language of your subconscious…Breathe…Smile.

25

Breathe normally. What is your very best childhood memory? Re-create the moment. This means that you are staying in the now; do not "go back" into that moment. Re-create, intensify, and empower its effect on you. Childhood's best memories are moments where we *know* life. It is the same as knowing a friend…You can trust that there will always be love. Breathe…Embrace life as you cherish a friend…Breathe…Sleep.

26

Breathe…In your awareness of the present moment, willingly participate in the rhythm of your breath. Govern the direction of your breath inside your body as you inhale and its journey out of your body as you exhale. This is an embrace of life. Have a grateful relationship with breath.

27

Breathe…Understand that you are moving. Things around you are constantly moving.

This is life…constant creation…Let yourself be moved by the cosmic creating and expanding movement. Inhale deeply and expand your belly and exhale…You are in perfect harmony with the universe. Feel it rocking you to sleep…Breathe deeply…

28

The universe understands and responds by giving you more of what you give to others.

29

Experience the gentleness of slow breathing. It will slow down your thinking and help relieve tension in your nerves and muscles. The best ideas do not come from brainstorms, but rather from the echo of the great cosmic vibrations you are connected to. Tune in, breathe, and let go…

30

Get into a sound mental and emotional state of mind. What will be already is. Breathe the world you want to see. Inhale powerfully, and exhale all the way till there is no air left. Repeat a few times, and then breathe normally; smile…

31

Lie down, keep it simple, and make it easy to fall asleep. Invest delight into your voluntary breaths. Enjoy already the steps you will take, and visualize where you will be when you reach your goal. Allow yourself this free time…Smile…Breathe…Go get your dream…

32

Use the motion of the wave to feel your breath. Breathe the air way down into your belly, fill it up, and exhale gently. Breathe in for the love of your life, and breathe out for the love of all lives. Let go…Let all this love surround you and your loved ones…

33

Learn to build a chain of moments with a chain of breaths. Create a direction for your thoughts so that you can act according to what you know to be right for you, and get your life to make sense. Tend to your inner life with love. Enjoy these last moments of the day…

34

Use the power of detachment to empower courage, not to validate ignorance. Use your power of flexibility to get through to the heart of what matters and enjoy a peaceful sleep…Be fine with who you are. Sleep, angel, sleep…

35

Accept things as they are. You don't have to agree with everything. Accept yourself as you are. You are beautiful. Breathe, and let it be.

36

Notice how smoothly and gracefully peaceful thoughts operate changes. You are becoming a well of inspiration as you dig deeper into your heart. Breathe consciously, and celebrate life as you surrender…

37

Breathe in fresh air. Breathe fresh thoughts. Thoughts become energy. They become reality. Prepare your sleep with the most wonderful thoughts, and let them go. Then let yourself go…

38

Let yourself rest…Repeat: "I rest comfortably in my open heart." Breathe…Sleep…

39

All the good deeds of the day, all the efforts to do right, all the love you gave from your heart will take you deeper into the wealth of your essence…Sleep deeply.

40

Go to your haven. Bring your presence into a beautiful forest where the moon rays light up your way toward the far, but bright, morning light…Sleep.

Short Texts to Take to Your Meetings — Breathe and Meditate

Remember that you access a different depth of knowledge if you read and write. I suggest you take time to copy a text and take it to your meeting to meditate upon as you breathe.

Conscious breathing is becoming your new habit. Habits create events. It will put people and opportunities that will fit with your ideal vision of life on your path.

Your mind needs food for thought. Your stomach needs good fuel to change your food into energy, and it needs a break between meals. Drink water. Give the word "hungry" a new definition and live by it. Be hungry for all that supports physical and spiritual life.

Tune in to your heart and tune up your breath and let the creative waltz of life carry you through the day.

Breathe, and empower yourself with every step as you harmonize the rhythm of breath with your movements…Create your elegance! See a beautiful universe in everyone you meet!

A moment lasts forever since it is part of the next one and the next one…

Choose a humanitarian cause to support today in your meeting with breath. Breathe in the courage of those who are actively working for that cause. Exhale, and cherish all the suffering people. This kind of compassion comes from deep inside. It will keep you in touch with what really matters. Then pick up the courage to put the half smile back on, and have the humility to go back to your daily chores.

Love your freedom. Become kinder and more flexible. Let others have the freedom to think what they want and to believe what they believe. This is a favorable way to appreciate your own freedom.

How you look at the world outside and how you care for your inner world melt into each other, and you create the world you see…

In one moment you use all the knowledge that you have accumulated in your lifetime so far. Always update it.

Becoming a powerful person is to choose to use your powers over yourself.

Engage in the changes you want to see in your life by changing one thing about the way you eat in the morning. Add a food that's alive, and take out something processed…or sit quietly to eat, or do not eat in the car. Cut down on coffee. You know what to do!

You know where you are heading. You have the power to get there smiling. Let there be peace and harmony in all facets of your being. This will make all the difference in whether you enjoy the ride or not.

To be able to meditate, you need to know the way you process your thoughts and to find the habit that is in place. When thoughts are observed, the emotion that backs them up shies away. Practice this, and you will meet with this stillness.

Let the waves of emotions smoothly and lovingly push you forward, and keep your eye on your destination.

Many powers become available once you are familiar with the way you process your thoughts, so you can use them favorably.

The key to a peaceful mind is to focus on breath, and let the thought process launder itself out as you entertain one thought that is of a more powerful quality than the zillion others.

Presence allows all the experiences that you have accumulated to sort themselves out and fall into an order that serves you.

Each person's reality is the reflection of where his or her presence is anchored.

If your awareness is mostly of the appearance, your reality is in what things appear to be.

Value beauty; work your way through to support kindness and freedom for all beings.

Work hard on yourself; you are fine-tuning some raw material, educating your emotions, and harnessing your mind's reactions.

Feeling more and more love? Do not fear that much love…It is only a glimpse of what you are capable of!

Express your love for nature and its offerings for a healthy mind and body. Stretch your mind out; breathe the freedom of the moment. This is where happiness lives. Breathe, and raise your energy level way up!

Part 4
Power of the Observer

Intentional breathing brings you into the moment. When you get out of the time zone that rules everything around you, you are creating a moment in your own space where you can observe yourself, your situation, your attitude, and your reactions. This is where you see the gap between what you value and how you live. Be a favorable observer.

This will help you move toward your dream, because you will value every conscious step you take toward it. If you want more peace, you will respond more peacefully. If you want more love, you will respond more lovingly.

Do not hesitate to raise your own standards, and dream big! You will learn a lot more.

Know Your Self

The first step you take in the morning is on the soil of that place inside, where you must stand and look around with a favorable perspective at what your life is and how it can grow. You need that step inside to get a fresh perspective. From there you can clearly see what you are about. This is the beginning of a relationship with yourself… an honest discovery and acceptance of your imperfections and deficiencies, and a recognition of your talents and your qualities.

This is also where you get a glimpse of what keeps you from believing in yourself and in your dreams. Through breath and presence, you will find your way through it. When you are walking and breathing, present to your heartbeat, you cut through the outside energies, events, or people who would otherwise alter your direction and mind your authority.

Believing in your dreams is the key to enjoying and putting to use your talents and your qualities, so that you can actively work toward the realization of those dreams.

Your favorable and empowering observer becomes the cornerstone of your new habit. A favorable observer will take more space and occupy more time in your daily life as your relationship develops. It is the sponsor of your life artistry. You will love having him around!

Go inside where your dreams are alive! Love is a pure healing force. It generates a favorable vision of yourself, of others, and of all life. Breathing with gratitude for life immediately opens the mind to a favorable perception.

Free your thoughts, and they will all gather in your divine intention—who you were meant to evolve into. Breathe these creative thoughts, and your intention will run freely through you.

Your observer echoes the messages from your inner voice, gently and tenderly. Life-force, God, or your angel guides you…They will not pick you up when you fall because the fall itself is a gift… It contains a lesson. Like the child who falls when learning to walk, playfully get back up, have a good laugh, and go on.

Part 5
The Powers behind Breath

You can turn the darkest hour into the greatest life lesson at the very moment it happens.

Your most important relationship is with breath. Conscious and mindful breathing brings awareness of the experience you are having. Presence is the power to relate to what you are experiencing. What you experience will be powerful and significant only if you have a relationship with it!

If a great opportunity knocks but presents itself as an annoying inconvenience in the moment, you can just pass right by, and save yourself the hassle…Or take a voluntary, mindful breath at that same moment, slow down, and pay attention to how you are relating to this event…frustration, or lack of interest? Through voluntary breathing the power of presence tells you that you might discover that the situation requires your attention in order to help you get a new perspective on a particular subject, and, therefore, give you the opportunity to expand your knowledge of yourself and expand your consciousness at the same time. One thing is for sure; it will teach you to open your mind enough to see what you might otherwise reject so hastily. This is how life-force works; you find the treasures along the way. Open up these moments; they are gifts!

In one moment of full presence you use many powers.

You have skills to develop. When this is done, these skills become powers, and they serve you in your daily life. They become a major part of any success.

Power Chain:
A Thought-Processing Habit
to Develop Using Your Powers

So let's see how these powers can link up and become a creative, happiness-oriented thought process.

A mindful thought process is all about following your breath inside to your heart and values… Get to *presence,* and then use the next power… *Detach* from all outer influence…to the next power…

That will become a new thought-processing habit, a healthy and beautiful one. This is how the chain works:

From *presence* you have a clear vision of the situation. You then…

Detach from outside events, and follow your breath inside to your own values so you can use your…

Self-authority, because when detached you have enough perspective to feel your freedom of choice. But you need to use…

Flexibility to allow yourself to be at ease with whatever is…so you can better explore your choices while embracing your…

Stability to stay within your values without interference from outside influence. All through this process you have…

Endurance, the ability to maintain the intensity of the now, to stay in the moment with…

Love, which changes your desire for things or people to be different than what or who they are, to acceptance of what *is*, and, therefore…

You *change* the outcome of the event.

Stillness is the overtone that allows all these skills to become powers.

All this in one breath!

Power of Presence

Voluntary, mindful breathing awakens an awareness of the self…being in the moment, now, in this breath. This is presence. A favorable presence takes the direction of the heart's calling. Presence will show you first who you are. It will first shed light on whether you are a favorable observer or a criticizing one, of yourself first, of others, and of life.

When we are fully present to our purpose, our values, and our goals, we do see more clearly how we act and react in different situations. We do see how we could have done it differently. Keep a good sense of humor. You might see yourself doing some pretty stupid things…Well, don't we all.

If you are not a favorable observer, you drift away from the present moment, holding on to thoughts that take you into an emotion that takes control and maintains your world in a frame that prevents it from expanding. You are not really holding the thought; you are holding your life so that it fits a restricted mind, and the moment it is out of that frame, you cannot access it.

Dare to step forward and recognize all of the possibilities that are there for you! Your mind expands naturally, and so does the entire universe. In your presence align your body with your heart and spirit, and use breath to connect to your vital life-force, and anchor yourself to your heart so you don't drift away.

This whole process is based on freedom of choice, and the choices are: either your world stagnates around your inferior self and the miscellaneous bits and pieces of each day, or your world turns, expands, and gives your superior *self* space to breathe!

The power of presence dwells in love. All the rest is only control, without any real power. This is self-discovery! You will find yourself being a great human being at times and less so at other times. You will have the power right then and there to breathe the whole thing into a new experience, and make your *now* count.

Power of Stillness

When you become present, you are aware of your tendencies to react to the world outside, and your senses are strongly solicited from all directions. This is when you must focus on your breath, and intentionally inhale peace, quietude. Breathe the fresh air in, and open your heart now.

The power of stillness transforms energies at the entrance of the heart. Compassion and love filter whatever is coming at you. Stay aware of your main activity. You are breathing; you are anchored, strong yet gentle. Your mind is like a castle, and the king or queen (presence) rules over his or her subjects (your thoughts). Stillness is when your kingdom is a place where everything is in order; everything is fine whatever the weather…

Stillness is gently resting your mind on your heart.

Power of Detachment

From stillness, you can detach from any outer situation and be neutral about the outcome of that outer event, because you are also detached from your emotional body and still firmly anchored, away from the busy shore. As you are breathing mindfully, fully present to your inner stillness, you elevate yourself above as a detached element of the scene being played; you are a neutral observer. You do not react, and you can clearly see the solution to any inner or outer conflict.

Power of Endurance

Maintaining the intensity level becomes easier with practice. I learned with kundalini yoga how to maintain a position past the pain, past the boredom, past any excuse I could find. Emotions are what usually stop us from maintaining this intensity. This is one of the main ingredients of the practice of the *now*. The intensity is the fire that pulsates to keep this moment alive. Creation needs fire…

As you continue developing your skills, you will find great support from your favorable observer, who will support you in this particular practice—because endurance makes you strong.

Staying present, detached, and persevering becomes easier. Your body and your mind are acquiring stability.

Power of Stability

This power is strongly felt by everyone around, as well as yourself. This is when your training really takes a turn. You have adopted conscious, intentional breathing as a habit that will replace attitudes and habits that will now start to fade away. As you pause to take a breath, your magnetic field is charged with the truth of your intention. Many desire this power; it is the essence of charisma. Remember, your intention is not yours; it is the intention life has for you. You are just a firm believer that life has great opportunities for you in store. Your projection is powerful, and people feel safe around you because once you master this skill, you realize that your heart is not so cluttered by fears and worries of all sorts, and kindness and love come through naturally. You will then be blessed with the power of self-authority.

Power of Self-Authority

Breathing mindfully, being present and detached, holding on to awareness, and being stable give you self-authority. Once you are in a position where you have the sense that you are free to live up to your own set of values, you will know how to respond to any event. You have freed yourself of reactions that pulled you down to values that are not up to your standards.

Self-authority and breathing in firmly are reminders that you and you alone are responsible for your choices, your attitude, and your behavior.

Self-authority will bring you grace and elegance of movement, physically and mentally, like a flow of life going in and out of you that nothing can disturb. This allows flexibility.

Power of Flexibility

Self-authority maintains awareness of your freedom of choice in any situation. The power of flexibility is a power that is used to free others as well as yourself. Being present, detached, and able to observe life events and persevere allow for stability and self-authority. This authority is so precious that you honor the authority of others over their own lives. Even if you totally disagree, you give them the freedom to be who they are in that moment. Power of flexibility organizes the negative energies around you so that they do not collide with your freedom. You are then participating in individual and collective healing.

When you are flexible in the *now*, all outer influences act on you as currents. In a river there are undercurrents that sometimes go in the opposite direction of the main flow. Flexibility is like water; with presence, you stay with the main flow.

Power of Love

Love is an art. Unless we have been blessed with genius at birth, art is something we have to learn and practice by developing particular skills.

But we are born out of love. Life always thrives on love. We know only love from the get-go!

There are zillions of ways to love. Love is all inclusive. There is one Love.

The art of *love* is an ongoing process. You have to be *present to the art of love.*

Love is the inner reflection of the half smile you wear.

When the heart is supported, heard, and free, it speaks only of *love.*

The power of *love* is all about healing the heart through connection with universal life-force. Breathe with love. We manifest love through love, happiness through happiness, joy through joy!

You are now manifesting health and beauty by healing your heart and learning your skills.

When in need of a boost, a lift…*love*. Give love. Manifest love.

Love your experience, whatever it might be. It has been designed by your superior *self* for you. Love and trust each moment.

Empower Yourself

Becoming a powerful person is to choose to use your powers over yourself. You are responsible for every food you feed yourself and others; every single thought reaches a destination. Practice breathing loving thoughts; empower them when inhaling, and exhale to send them on their destination.

You have to prepare for a change—any change you make will affect all facets of your life! If you think that you can change the way you relate to others without changing the way you relate to yourself, you will give up and think that nothing works for you!

The first thing that needs to be clear in love is your perception of yourself. Your perception of life comes from how you love yourself.

Are your dreams built on values that support their manifestation? Are you living up to these values? How do you perceive your dreams? Make sure your definition of dream includes the word "reachable." Make sure to believe a little more every day in your dream!

Conscious, voluntary breathing is using the power to find the strength and courage to wake ourselves up and empower our dreams on this side of life.

One step at a time is the only way to get steady enough to pick up speed and maintain the course. Keep it simple, and be grateful every step of the way.

Voluntary breathing as your first step of the day is like turning on the switch to light up the journey's itinerary.

The change starts as soon as you take your first mindful breaths. Take your time. Bring all your attention to your first voluntary breath of the day…of your meeting…You will feel like you are putting a key into a lock that hides a great deal of love. This love alone can fix all your problems.

This first breath gives you the opportunity to check out your "heart place" from a different perspective. You will find the way to your values, and you will find new ways to integrate them more and more into your life

Your higher values have been waiting below the horizon of your heart. In opening your heart, the quality of your thoughts will rise and join your most elevated vision, which will then match your commitment to your personal evolution and support you.

Your awareness in breath and the depth of your practice as you work toward a great, healthy, and beautiful life is equal to your interest in life, and it is up to you to make it interesting!

Part 6
My Experience with Breath

*A mindful breath and an inspired
thought are the only tools you
need to become an alchemist.*

I died one early morning, some years ago. I remember my last breath as I was fighting for my life. I inhaled with all the strength I had left in me. Some force came in and assembled every moment of my life experience, going t every part of my body, and pulled every single one of them out of my physical being. I was holding on to that breath…but I was going along with this life stream that was not mine. I stopped and had a look at the motionless body.

I, as I knew myself, was taken out of the equation. I was not going along with this life stream—I was it. Everything I had experienced in my life, everything I knew and all that I had done—all of that was taken out of "me" and became some kind of magnetic form that fit in a space that was pulling me in.

I was purifying in the fire of the speed of light. Only some parts of my life remained, and that was all that made an imprint, like a password or a key.

Everything that had been carried from me to "there" had been transformed. There was an exchange—a gift—that still unveils itself more and more every day of my life.

I was sent back. I saw my body from light-years away. It was a space that was expecting me. I was coming in full speed, going through layers and layers of massive collective consciousness, all made of the remains of different levels of mindfulness… forces that are built during lifetimes, places I had shed some of my life experience. I went through what I saw as the consciousness that now thrives to rule over the earth, and I knew then I would have to tell the whole world, everyone, to build in themselves the power of love, to love as much as they can so that the power of love grows and becomes the ruling consciousness. Always promote love. Always remember love.

I was a life-force coming to animate that body and create through it. I would learn through it, and I would teach through it.

I went in and passed through the lungs, and I went down the diaphragm and into the belly to fill it to full capacity…and the body trembled and choked, and it exhaled me and coughed me away, and I had to push through again to go into lungs that were gasping for air in violent moves. I pushed and entered again and again, until it took me in and settled down.

A sound of drums welcomed me; the heart found its rhythm. The blood flushed through the veins like a waterfall; the spirit harmonized the whole process. My mind was open wide, and this life was connected to the life-force of the universe.

I realized later that all this had happened between an inhale and an exhale…I came back with the knowledge that I *am* a life-force that will live way past this lifetime.

To me this is an infinite energy. It is not there to answer to us, to our demands. We are here to embody this cosmic consciousness.

We can be part of the elevation or the depression of collective consciousness while human. The entrance into the next realm does not have to be a strange place. We can breathe the essence, the soul of the perfect life energy, right *now*.

The energy that we are now will continue. We will get more of what we give. Giving love every time we can and living in gratitude are the most important investments we can ever make.

Breathing was part of my healing process after this event. I lived one breath at a time, for a long healing period. It is amazing how life is precious when you receive and host it consciously. One breath becomes the now and one now follows another and they all become the now of life, one long moment versus a fast life between moments that matter.

There was no sense of time in my out-of-body experience. Time is an earthly invention that fills agendas and too often prevents us from seeing and considering living in real time, with the real clock that ticks inside each of us—the cosmic time of natural cycles.

There is no final breath. I will never "fight" for my life again because whether the experience is happening here or not, it goes on. I sometimes see it as someone fighting to stay in the same grade at school so he does not lose his friends or change teacher! We live to become the life-force that we build while experiencing our lifetime here. It is so extremely important to remember this in the choices we make and the kind of force we want to teach to others.

There is no need to fight in life but a great need to become a loving and favorable spirit while alive. This world greatly needs each of us to work harder on spreading love around. More, more, more love…the more we give, the more we have!

This was my own experience. I feel good believing this. I have no choice; it is imprinted in my heart.

Make sure whatever your beliefs are that you use your freedom and self-authority to act upon them. Express what you believe in, your values, without any fear. Your beliefs are right for you, and another's beliefs are fine for another's given destiny. There are truths to be discovered and love to be experienced all along the way for each one of us. We need to accept each other for who we are and what we know. Since we do what we know…we need to be eternal students of wisdom so we keep on doing better and better.

Part 7
Short Meditations to Reflect Upon

Breathe to feed your heart, to open your mind, and to accept who you are. Inhale in a bigger version of life! Exhale with gratitude for your ever-expanding evolution.

Breathe in the stability of the mountain. Breathe in the fragility of the young sprouted seed growing through rocks and the strength of the tree.

In a storm breathe in the force of the thunder…of the winds…and of the lightning. Breathe in the power of the elements, not the fear of it.

Breathing is a voluntary act, even if we do have a backup system that takes over when needed. We have been given the freedom to choose. You change the moment when you stop relying on the automated system and intentionally assume the responsibility of your very own life-support system! This brings you back to your divine presence, your own center, to the experience of your life.

On this journey there will be obstacles. Life-force will place them right in front of you, breaking the image that you have of yourself to free your true identity.

Breathe, and bring you presence in full awareness of a much larger world and a much bigger inner life. Take the frame out of your perception of life, and experience the *self* that has no limits.

In your relationship with your *self*, all solutions will show up in your mind's eye. Be present; from there it is a matter of time before the material support shows up at your door.

In a few weeks, stepping up to a higher level of mindfulness will be so attractive to you it will seem that you will be accepting an invitation instead of maintaining a discipline!

Expand your mind to include all that your eyes cannot see, and your heart will beat to the sound of the universal rhythm. Open your door and enter the eternal creative energy. Offer your contribution. Breathe who you are, an infinite part of it all.

Visualize your breath. See it join your thoughts. Check out how it circulates inside your body as you breathe in. Infuse your breath with vitality, and see your love and care embracing every inch of it.

Breathe out, and visualize your breath as your contribution to the world you want to see. Cherish all children of all ages…Cherish the life that is thriving through thick and thin. Remember the sprouting seed growing through rocks… Participate in the flow of strength and courage that it needs. Love and care for everyone and every inch of this planet…every ray of light of this universe. Stay with the bigger picture.

Whatever is going on in your life, you do not have to take it all as a packaged deal, where the meaning, the emotion, and the reaction are all included in your usual perception of things, generating the same reactions over and over when you wish you would just respond differently.

You are getting some new tools. A voluntary breath with conscious, sincere desire to get to new horizons will provide you with the vision you need to not react anymore, but act upon your heart's calling.

Fast changes for quick results disconnect mind, body, and heart. You push the heart aside and go with your brains, or vice versa. You cut off the spirit and go with the heart—let's say you decide to stop eating sweets—without aligning your body, mind, and spirit. What happens? Your heart will soon say, "Oh, I need comfort food." Your brain cannot stop your heart's desire, so it will answer, "Go for it, just for today; comfort food is a good thing," and your spirit will feel let down. Oh, the dialogues we have that we do not hear!

Conscious breathing and awareness assign the meeting of the body, mind, and spirit to a place of honor in your life. It is then that your mind naturally sets sail, the heart beats with joy, and the winds start blowing your way. Your spirit guides you as you cut smoothly into the waves of change. Nothing is disconnected; everything works together. All energies head in the same direction, toward the same goal.

According to Einstein, "We cannot solve our problems with the thinking we used to create them." The only requirements to access the power of *presence* are your honesty and your willingness to come face-to-face with who you really are. This power runs on the fuel of love and kindness. You can look at yourself honestly without judging yourself.

All this power is in the breath. You are here, now, beautiful and healthy, and all is fine. You are present in the *life-force*, with a half smile on your face, and all is in order.

The *power* of *presence* is the first gift that you receive from intentional, mindful breathing. If you learn to use it, other gifts follow. In this process one power supports the next one. Such is the art of *life*.

In conscious breathing we find out just how perfectly our human and divine nature can create health and beauty. The mind, the body, and the spirit must support each other and be one. Changes are made based on personal values; it is all about what we believe life should be. Social values often interfere with our own value system.

Everything we do should represent our own beliefs…the tone of our voice, the way we walk, the way we see and treat each other. There is a truth that reigns over our human behavior. Lasting changes are built on high values.

This is where the true choice is. This is the real challenge. What you want to see in your life lets your set of values rise to your conscious presence, and either you raise your expectations, or you disempower yourself with excuses or by habit. Go for your full potential. It will work. It will be a trip! You are a full universe. Explore! You will find your way…and mostly, enjoy the ride.

Think of Atlas, condemned to carry the world on his shoulders for eternity. This is what many are doing—supporting causes they don't believe in, living with a constant weight on their shoulders, condemning themselves. Put the world as you know it down, and walk away.

Breathe, and be present to your ideal world. Be still. Be present to the possibilities and opportunities that are coming your way. Let that presence permeate your whole being.

Create the world you want to see every morning. This cycle is starting clean. Unlike Atlas, free your heart, free your mind, and free your hands so you can pick up some flowers along the way!

Let Thy Food Be Thy Medicine

Breathe in the beauty of the yellow and orange foods that contain alpha- and beta-carotene. When assimilated, the body converts yellow and orange foods into vitamin A, which is vital to the maintenance of the lining of the respiratory, urinary, and intestinal tracts; it is a very powerful support for the immune system, eyes, skin, and bones. It slows aging.

Learn about the alchemy that happens inside your body. Get into this fascinating, magical universe of transformation that makes you who you are. Food for the body affects the mind and the heart…Food for thought affects your body, your health, and your beauty!

Explore the body and its functions. Explore the plants that support them. Explore music as food for the heart. There is so much to enjoy in the learning of life and the art of living! Never stop learning. Everything is food.

Food Is Energy

The body speaks to us. It speaks through the energy we feel when we rise in the morning. To better hear it, there is yoga. We enter into a conversation with the body by stretching it, by using every muscle and strengthening every nerve. We get intimate at the cellular level; we feed it oxygen, and we bless it as it carries our consciousness through life.

The food we eat generates and defines the energy that we feel as we rise. It is the essence of nature that is at work in our biological system transforming into an attitude that supports uplifting thoughts, love and joy or heavy depressing negative thought processing. Make sure you eat food that is fresh and alive. Engage with the colors that will fill your magnetic field with radiant, powerful energy and share with all you meet.

You Talk to Your Food—The Inner Dialogue

There isn't anything new in talking to our food. We do it all the time. Everyone does it, but it is more of a monologue, or a skin-deep conversation, as the tongue says, "I really, really feel like having you…" The eyes see it, and that's it… got to have it…eat it…"Yum! That tasted good!" Over and done.

When you care to know what a certain food can do for you, you deepen the relationship, and you orchestrate your plate with intention. You may need a high of energy for the next day—to run a marathon, for example—or you might want to spend a day contemplating nature and eat light food. Your mind and your body get together with your heart's intention. You must tune in and use food that will enhance your experience.

When going to the food store, train your mind's eye to link up the colors of food with your energy. Your desire to eat this or that will speak to you differently.

Part 8
Value of Health and Beauty, For Centering Thoughts

The practice of voluntary breathing awakens the awareness of your powers.

Consciously breathing healthy and beautiful thoughts is more powerful than any diet or any cosmetic you could ever use to feel beautiful and healthy.

Our value of health does not express itself only by what is on our food plates. It defines the quality of everything that we feed our body, our mind, and our spirit.

A painter, Jean-Francois Millet, represents the high values of healthy food in a painting called *The Angelus*. A man and a woman farmer are depicted in the fields at the break of day, heads bent and hands joined, connecting with life-force before working the soil to create a food garden. You can feel this moment of prayer as a humble offering. Everything is still…You can almost hear them breathe.

This connection is the real food for body, mind, and spirit. We do not have to be out in the fields, but we can take a moment to breathe some gratitude and offer our day's work in the morning. Watering the soil of our heart and listening to its beat is also mental and spiritual food. Getting in harmony with all life's creation feeds the body, the mind, the heart, and the spirit.

When food is on the table—even if the ingredients are of the highest quality—the thought of the earth, of the young sprout that emerges from the seed, the flower that came before the fruit, seeing the journey of the gardener or the farmer, and smiling at whoever shares the meal with you…these are the most nourishing parts of the meal. This is conscious eating. What is on your plate is what would result if you had used your hands yourself to grow this food or care for the animals if you were in the fields. Or maybe what you feed yourself does not inspire life…and even less important to you is where it was produced. Then your mind separates from your heart. You are not in touch with what you value.

The food you are eating should be in harmony with the beauty that you see, or would like to see, in the world. What is beautiful about the food you eat? The smile of the local farmer? That is spiritual food. The care for the earth? Food for the heart. You feed from every ion of energy that is contained in anything that you digest. Healthy digestion is linked with your recognition of an attitude toward your beliefs about what beauty is and how you participate in it.

Earthly foods and celestial foods are the basis of the perfect diet for the body, the mind, and the spirit for maximum health and infinite beauty! Listen to your heart's guidance.

Conscious eating is like conscious breathing; it is food for every living cell in and out of your body.

Beauty Is in the Eye of the Beholder

Our perception is a print, a copy of what we have learned. Generations have different perceptions because they learned about life a different way from the outside world.

From the inside world, our needs as human beings have always been the same: freedom and love.

Our spirit is like a freelance designer who does not have established rules!

Our perception is original if we look with our heart. Then we can only create and generate new, fresh energy!

Just watch two musicians playing the same tune with the same instrument. One plays with soul; his eyes are closed, and the music runs freely through him from his heart. The other is reading a music sheet. One goes by his own rules. He plays an original version every time! The other plays someone else's original version. Once he allows love and freedom to flow and breathes with self-authority, it will empower his skill, and he will dare create his own version!

In order to do that, he will need to erase from his mind the belief that he can only follow the notes that are written, let his spirit free, and use his talent, which his whole being will generate from inside. Through practice, he will get there.

The complex organization that took place to structure our lives today presented us with images that altered our perception of life itself. Everything has been engineered so that we have to do but we do not have to be. Our perception of life is now about what things life has to offer. We must go inside to reach the true essence of life and offer who we are. Just take more time to be and not do so much.

Living in the moment is observing what is inside of ourselves, editing the outside world with the language of the heart, based on our own value system. Living in a moment that is taking you out of yourself and printing depressing or exciting messages in your heart is not living your life; it is giving away your moments.

The choice that you have to perceive beauty and health in all that you see cannot be taken away from you. That is your self-authority. Your perception of the moment is what makes it *your* moment. When heaviness sets in, ask yourself:

Is there another way I could look at this person or event? The answer should be: yes, it is only up to me.

Know that life challenges you only to the degree of your capacity. The bigger the challenge, the more life is telling you what you are capable of.

The most perfect face does not represent health or beauty if it is without an easy and honest smile. The most beautiful body does not represent health or beauty if it lacks grace and elegance of movement. Breathing consciously and entertaining loving and caring thoughts toward yourself and others will give you a glow and radiance that cannot come from the outside.

Breath and Communication

The universe is expanding. Your mind—the channel that allows the deepest communication with all that exists, from the most profound to superficial matters—is also in constant expansion. Mindfully inhale deeply to communicate with your body on a cellular level. The more profound the communication, the more intuitive your mind gets. Breathe with spirit, and direct freedom to your heart's intention.

Use your freedom of choice, and trust in your self-authority.

Intentionally breathe when you come into a situation that presents a skin-deep communication, and be present to who you are. Be present to the effect of the words you speak and the words you hear on your heart and spirit. If it is uplifting, engage. Be mindful of where you direct the sound of your voice. Address the heart, and people will listen. Address the ears, and they will only hear. Address the brains, and they will argue. And don't forget—not everything has to be serious! Belly laughs are charged with healing energy, and communicating joy is important.

By using the power of *presence*, you are becoming aware of things that have become obsolete for you. You are aware that to stay present to such a communication will drain you. Be grateful. You are seeing the true you. Act upon it, but remember to always be kind and compassionate to others as you are to yourself.

Mindful Breathing

The first step in mindful breathing is about greeting and accepting who you are each and every morning, and stretch that moment of intense inner power through the day. Your first voluntary breath of the morning is your starting point, and there is only *one* way to go from there. We all want to be happy, healthy, and beautiful. Mindful breathing will allow you to see your own thoughts by clearing your mind and doing a serious cleanup in your thought-processing file. Just breathe, and open your mind to who you are, all of you. Accept every inch of your body and every beat of your heart. Accept your relationship with life as it is now. Take your time, and create perfectly balanced moments into a developing relationship that is loving and enjoyable. Accept that they are but individual moments, and know that you are now learning to use more and more conscious moments to be happy.

Breathing presence and awareness with a favorable attitude change your mind's orientation toward your heart's contentment.

The practice of mindful breath provides the sensation of bathing in a world where there is nothing unresolved, no questions pending. Everything just is.

Definition of Habit

A habit is a mechanism that has slowly made a home in your subconscious in order for you to get through an experience. It develops and creates its own way of putting thoughts together so that that you need to feel you are equipped to take on the challenge. That need is backed up by an emotional behavior that supports or validates the need for the experience.

But what happens when the challenge is over? You will never win if you do not put down the arms. Whatever the event, whatever pain or sorrow it may have caused you, be grateful for the way you got yourself through and came out strong, with a new look on life: the look of the warrior that put down the arms because the battle is over. Peace becomes the only goal.

Old habits die hard, we say. Not so. Habits are supported by emotions. They are supported by memories only you can keep alive and give power to or turn into great experiences for you to meet victory.

Breathing voluntarily with gratitude for every new day will give your emotions a place where they can work for you, not against you.

Once they become useful, your emotions will support the flow of energy that wants to create new habits—good, healthy, beautiful habits.

The Healer

The healer is one who accepts everything as good and finds a rightful place for each event in life. Everything that life-force creates and instills in someone has an intention. That intention is always part of an evolution. Whatever the event, however difficult, it is always equal to the capacity of the one who experiences it. Healing is all about being ready and willing to relate to a mental, physical, or emotional challenge and not be its victim.

Many look at illnesses as battles to fight. It seems to be a way to gather energy and say yes to life. These are thoughts that have traveled through human minds for centuries. The healer is never a fighter; he is all about love. Do not fight the thoughts that keep coming back to pain you; let them be useless in the new *now* of your life.

Intentional, conscious, deep breathing with the powers of presence, detachment, perseverance, stability, and flexibility is a process. Smile, and enjoy watching the details, but keep your eye on the big plan always. The healer does.

Part 9
In Conclusion

You have now learned the ABCs of peace of mind. Apply all that you have practiced every day, and you will master it.

Meditation becomes simple when our thoughts are eager to feed on health and beauty.

Take notes! Fill your time differently. Start a thirty-minute food exploration on the Internet or in books…Check the source of information, open your mind, and choose to go an alternative way than your usual beliefs…Dare to feel and think differently!

You just need to stay present to the health and beauty that comes from the heart, so it will become the world you see. When thoughts manifest, they just become what is. We are then in the true essence of life, thoughtless.

Take a few minutes every day to sit on the ground, or in a chair, and practice going inside and being who you aspire to be. In the multitude of choices, keep it simple.

See a bird on a branch...Hear him sing... See the tree...See the blue sky above...Hear the leaves, and feel the warm breeze flowing... See the clouds passing...See the bird fly away... Follow him... Be the bird. Dare to be who you are at your best, at all times.

There are so many simple ways to create beautiful moments, to change a reality that pulls your energy down. Ascend. Look up. Elevate. Stand tall, and breathe powerfully.

Part 10
Journaling, a writing journey to wholeness

Day 1

Day 2

Day 3

Day 4

Day 5

❖❖❖

Day 6

Day 7

Day 8

Day 9

Day 10

Day 11

Day 12

Day 13

Day 14

Day 15

❖ ❖ ❖

Day 16

Day 17

Day 18

Day 19

Day 20

Day 21

❖❖❖

Day 22

Day 23

Day 24

Day 25

Day 26

Day 27

Day 28

Day 29

Day 30

Day 31

Day 32

Day 33

❖❖❖

Day 34

Day 35

Day 36

Day 37

Day 38

Day 39

Day 40

www.ingramcontent.com/pod-product-compliance
Lightning Source LLC
Chambersburg PA
CBHW051651040426
42446CB00009B/1086